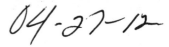

The Joy in the Morning and a New Day Begins

The Joy in the Morning and a New Day Begins

A Collection of Inspirational Poems

By

Doris Washington

Book Cover & Photographs By Joni Meyers
Interior Photograph of Chapter 2: My Child is supplied
By the Author

To order additional copies of this book, contact:
Xlibris Corporation
1-888-795-4274
www.Xlibris.com
Orders@Xlibris.com
102901

Contents

Through And Beyond The Storm

My Child

The Joy In The Morning

A New Day Begins

Accepting

God's Peace

In Due Season

Faith

Memories & Reflections

A Time, A Season, And Always Love

Dedication

I dedicate this book and give special thanks to my husband John. For his love and support helped make this work all possible.

I Thank God For You

Each day I thank God for You.
The joy you have given to me-
And still do.
The comfort I feel always you beside me.
I Thank God for You.

When we made that commitment
To love and to cherish each other,
No matter what comes our way
Says so much about our love.
I Thank God for You.

You're my partner—my friend.
And the blessing is that our love
Has surpassed through the years.
I Thank God for You.

Each day I thank God for many things.
But what I thank Him for the most-
Is the joy you have given to me-
And still do.
I Thank God for You!

Acknowledgements

I give special thanks to my husband John, my son John, and many friends and family.

To Lenore Wossidlo, Sue Dolan, Sue Brenner, Attorney James West Esquire, Attorney Barbara Ransom, Sarah Grant, Dee Thompson, Barbara Roopnaraine, Ernie Wilkerson, Dennis Debbaudt, Joy Marie Demetriou, Joni Meyers, and to my mother Emma Buchanan. Your support is greatly appreciated. For you helped make this creation all possible.

My Spiritual Journey

There are those circumstances and events that occur in one's life, and then all of a sudden that life takes a different turn. That happened to me. A most traumatic experience occurred in my life. And through it all I found a new life—*my walk with God.* It began one late afternoon in December 1993. It was not a very cold day. And I can remember most vividly there was no snow on the ground, only somewhat cloudy. My son John who was eighteen years old at the time was playing outside as he normally does.

John always had a set routine. And in the afternoon he would go outside and walk back and forth, and sometimes he would look inside the window to see if I would change the channel of his favorite TV show. On this particular day his routine was interrupted.

Two police officers not aware of his autism held him on the ground with handcuffs in the front yard of our home. John was injured with a separated shoulder. I was in such disbelief that this happened. This was the most crucial time in my life where I sought God's help and strength to get through. I needed God at that most difficult time.

Each day I would pray. I would begin to pray every morning, and most of the day. My son began to regress in school. I too had to have therapy. My husband and I found strength with the Grace of God. This was a time of great healing for my family. This was a storm we weathered through. And God was right there with us through it all.

It wasn't too long after that I went through the legal process seeking some sense of justice for John's unfair treatment. We did not prevail with the legal process. Even so, going through it I had felt a sense of relief to know I helped make it better so another incident would not occur. It's like a peace you feel when you work to right a wrong.

And regardless of the outcome you made it better for someone else. I joined with many organizations that represent persons with special needs in this effort.

We met with many legislators in the state. There were press conferences, TV, radio appearances, and newspaper coverage. Before I knew there were parent advocates as well as other organizations in our state and other states involved in this great effort. More and more I would hear of incidents that had occurred in my state and other states involving persons with special needs and police. The need was great. We were successful in developing a statewide program *Recognizing Special Needs* in the state of Pennsylvania. And now there are continuing updates on police training. More updates of police training and autism continued to develop. I began to heal as I pursued the quest for police training. John was beginning to heal too.

As I continued to pursue statewide police training, I would write inspirational poems. My poems became a great healing and inner peace that I have never known. And more than that my poems has been an inspiration to others. I somehow feel my advocacy work and my poetry have been greatly connected.

I first started to write poems sharing my personal experiences living with autism that expresses a positive side in how to look it at. I began to write poems about inner peace, my closeness with God, spirituality, inspiration, social issues, hope, love, positive thinking, and greetings. My poetry has been a great healing for me, and continues to be. And what I find most fulfilling is the inspiration behind my writing is my son. My personal experience living with autism has also connected me to writing more inspirational poems. And through my poetry I have been inspired to take my experiences of life's daily challenges and share it with others how to best live life with a positive attitude and finding God's peace through it all. I found the more I am at peace in how to live life more fulfilled, I am encouraging others to do so.

As I look back when the incident with my son occurred, I have found a new sense to live life more positive no matter my circumstance. May we all find that *Joy In The Morning And A New Day Begins.* And may we spread a little *Love* wherever we go.

Foreword

The Joy In The Morning And A New Day Begins is all about healing, positive thinking, joy, encouragement, inspiration, the awareness of autism, inner peace, faith, hope and love. In this collection I have combined a variety of poems, some old and many new ones for all to read. Along with the variety of poems, I also share what has inspired me to write. I share my story about a time that very much impacted my life greatly, that involved my son who has autism and two police officers, and how it empowered me to advocate for a statewide training program for police officers to be aware of and recognize persons with special needs.

As readers are given a variety of my poems, there is also the story behind my poems inviting readers to my world as a mother who lives with autism. Readers will be truly inspired by this collection of poems. In the poem *Thank You For This Day* I express about God's healing and that you can always begin again. Other familiar poems I have included are *Gathering Stones, A New Day, Accepting* and many more.

In the poem *The Child That Plays Alone* I invite you to my personal experiences living with autism, for a better understanding of my son's uniqueness and gifts. Also in this collection, I have a chapter of poems in dedication to family that includes: *Daddy, Bryan, and Mother I Thank you.* Along with the many variety of poems familiar ones such as *Don't Forget To Count Your Blessings, Blessings* and *The Lord's Grace,* and other poems I share about finding that "inner peace" that includes other poems: *God's Peace* and *The Joy In The Morning.* I also share poems about love and peace in the world that includes: *Only Love, Love, What Matters Is Love,* and *A Time, A Season And Always Love.*

As you read this collection of poems, may it inspire you to read over and over again, encourage you to share with others and bring you that *Joy In The Morning* we all long for to have every moment of each day.

Through And Beyond The Storm

Face each challenge and believe with faith.
Brighter days are just moments away.
For His promise is the reassurance
He'll see you through every storm and beyond.

Always There

You're always there though every trial,
Every triumph,
Your peace I find.
I lift my head up high,
Knowing my help comes from-
You.

I Praise you,
Every minute,
Every hour,
Every day.
For you're always there
Guiding me through it all.
Reassuring me so much.

You're my salvation,
My joy in the morning
To hold me as the evening comes,
And on to the next new day.

There's so much I can say about you.
Your goodness,
Your grace.
And I Thank you
To Know-
You're-
Always There.

Rising Above The Storm

The problems keep coming,
And don't seem to go away.
I feel so tired ready to quit,
And still I pray.
I pray to weather the storm
As the tide rises so high.
And when I know I've done all I can.
I find comfort to know that I tried.

So I Stand!
And I Stand!
For the Lord gives me strength to get through.
And when the days seem cloudy and gray,
I don't carry the blues.
So I pray,
And trust in the Lord to know
He'll always be there.
And as the tide rises so high,
My burdens are not heavy to bear.
Rising Above The Storm

As Tomorrow Comes

Hope may seem difficult to hold on to.
And whatever challenges you may
Experience at the present day,
Know it's a temporary thing.
For today may not be your tomorrow.

Hold on to the Hope when it seems
Difficult to do so.
Just Hold On.
And believe the sun will rise again.
Yes!
The sun will rise-
As Tomorrow Comes.

As You're Going Through

I can worry when things aren't what
They should be.
I can be stressed every minute,
Every hour of the day when problems arise.

I can feel my heart with anxiety when it seems
It's not getting better.
I can take my stress level to another level,
Angry, bitter and just feeling not so good at all.
Yet, I can see the sunshine through it all.
He's taught me that so very much.
And as I believe tomorrow will be better
Than I can ever imagine,
I'm at peace.

Gathering Stones

Recovering from it all,
I pick up the broken pieces along the way.
Drifting away far too long,
I now re-group to get some balance.
And I'm ready to begin again.

There's so much out here to discover.
And yet I feel uncertain where
I'm going.
Taking it one step at a time,
I seek the desires of my heart.
And my dreams are not far away
To be fulfilled.

Recovering from it all,
I pick up the scattered pieces along the way.
Drifting away—far too long,
I now re-group to get some balance.
And I'm ready to begin again.
Out Here-
Gathering Stones!

You

Silence after the Storm,
The Storm that was raging
So long.
The Storm is over now.
Time to start a new direction.
Time to find a new sense of purpose.
Leaving what is familiar,
Even with new ventures to seek.
The old will not be again.
And taking it one step at a time,
It will be alright.
For I'm here,
Alive like I never been before.
Thank you Lord-
I begin here!
I begin with-
You!

The Sunshine

When your day seems cloudy and gray.
Pray the Lord will take your blues away.
Just Look for the Sunshine

And before you know what's troubling you,
Will start to go away, and you're no longer blue.
Just Look for the Sunshine

For you decide how you live for whatever way
You choose.
And if your way of living is positive,
You have nothing to loose.
Just Look for the Sunshine

For if you wear a smile and not a frown,
You'll find many of life's challenges will not get you down.
Just Look for the Sunshine

Remember to keep the love in your heart.
For staying positive is the most important part.
Just Look For-
The Sunshine!

Through And Beyond The Storm

See the sun as the storm comes.
He brings hope through it all.
Hold on to it always.
Trust in Him.
He's always there.
Sometimes Life can bring
Many challenges.
Sometimes all at once.
And whatever comes to be,
Know it will pass.
Hold on,
And Pray.
For as the Storm comes,
Know He'll always be there-
Through And Beyond!

Praising You

I Praise you during the storm,
And after the storm has passed.
I Praise you when it seems no relief,
And for each blessing you bring.

I Praise you when the river overflows,
And when the sea is calm.
I Praise you when the world is not at peace,
And when peace is all around.

I Praise you when the rain seems to never end,
And when the sun shines so bright on any given day.

I Praise you for my trials,
And for the strength you give me each day.
I Praise you for prayers answered before and after.

I Praise you for letting me know
You're always there,
And for being my friend.

I Praise you for your guidance,
And for the reassurance that you bring.
I Praise you for the challenges,
And for that anchor as you see me through.

I Praise you for reminding me what you're
All about,
And for teaching me so much.
I Praise you for each and every day,
And for loving me as I am.
Dear Lord!
I cannot stop-
Praising You!

My Child

He is my joy, my inspiration in all I do.
For there're so many things
I can tell you about my child.
But there's just more thing I got to say-
My Child is everything in the world to me.

John

You are a precious child,
For you have been sent from God above.
You are the joy of my life.
For you have taught me how to Love.

You brighten up the day
With your everlasting smile.
I am so proud to have you as my son.
For you help make my life worthwhile.

As I hear your sweet melody of songs you sing.
It could be a spiritual or popular tune or too.
How beautiful and special you are.
For this is all-What Makes You!

You make my life worth living.
And I keep going each and everyday.
How Important You Are To Me—So true!
As I look forward to everyday.
And I hear you say: "God is with us."
And I respond: "All the time."
I could not imagine my life without you.
My Precious Son—
John

When December Comes

When December Comes-
He is not the same.
Memories of that "cold winter day"—
Are with him—*Again and Again.*

When December Comes—
He thinks about what happened to him.
As he played outside and they approached him.

When December Comes-
He remembers the "hurt and pain"—
He went through.
Years have come and gone,
And a little part of him is—"blue."

When December Comes-
He goes through it,
Adjusting—but not—"ok."
For his life has changed because of it.
And with Him it—stays.-
When December Comes

Do You See Him? Do You Hear Him? Do You Know Him?

Do You See Him?
He is my child.
And he is dear to me.
He has Autism—an *Invisible Disability.*

Do You Hear Him?
You may not understand
Why he does not quickly respond to you.
For he is not bad,
He is just different from what you are used to.

Do you Know Him?
You may find he will need more time
To do a certain task.

And if there are too many demands,
Please understand they may be difficult
For him to grasp.

For there are other places
I could have chose for him to live.
I made the choice for him to stay with me,
For I see what he can give.

He may not understand danger.
I worry if he will be safe.
And as I struggle with the many difficulties,
And challenges—"I Keep The Faith!"

I only ask for him—One Request!

Please Learn About Him.
So he can have a chance to give his *Best!*
Do You See Him? Do You Hear Him? Do You Know Him?

Tears

Many times for You I cry tears.
And I go on,
I Cry! I Pray!
To believe someday,
You'll have a place too!
Many times for You I cry tears,
When the world doesn't understand
All about you—I Cry! I Pray!
Hoping you will not waste away
With your beautiful soul,
That some don't always see.
Many times for You I cry tears.
When it's not easy to explain,
Why today you're not doing well,
And you can't express with words
How you feel.
Many times for You I cry tears.
For a great understanding of your
Uniqueness, and worth.
As I accept you exactly as you are—
I Cry! I Pray!
Others will too!

Many times for You I cry tears.
And I go on,
I Cry! I Pray!
To believe someday,
You'll have a place too!
Many times for You I Cry-
Tears.

Invisible

He is different.
Does that make him not important?
No!
For everything you don't understand
About Him,
Are things that only belong to him?

You see he gets excited at times with a great
Amount of energy.
What you don't see is that he sings with a melody
That only belongs to him.

You see him run.
What you don't see is that every year
He participates in Special Olympics-
The 50 yard dash.
It's such an event to see,
And it only belongs to him.

You may see him when he bangs and screams out.
What you don't see he likes to talk to you about
What clothes you may be wearing,
And he'll give you a friendly "hi"-
That only belongs to him.

Invisible to you.
That makes him different!
Because He Has Autism!

The Child That Plays Alone

He talks to himself and no one hears what he says.
His activity seems strange and unusual to some.

If only they would see his gift, he could accomplish
More than you know.
If only someone would take the time to explore
What he has.

He could be a great musician, a great artist, a great dancer-
A great athlete.
He has many toys and he plays by himself.
The other children do not understand him.
They do not play with him.

He likes to do the same things other children do.
And yet he is shut out from the world.
He is different, but aren't we all different.

If only someone would play with him.
If only someone would see His Gift!
The Child That Plays Alone

My Child

My Child may wander off in his own place.
My Child may seem distant,
And he likes his space.

My Child may not like a crowd.
My Child sometimes may be loud.

My Child may not like touch.
My Child may not respond and speak much.

My Child likes routine.
My Child also likes music, and to sing.

My Child may not run and play like other children do.
My Child likes the Special Olympics, and swimming too!

For there're so many things I can tell you
About my child-
Most Certainly!
But there's just one more thing I got to say-
My Child is everything in the world to me.
My Child!

I Beat At A Drum

I Beat At A Drum you're not familiar with.
For the Lord blesses each of us with a Gift.

I make a sound you may not understand.
I have the humbleness to be someone's friend.

I Beat At A Drum you're not familiar with.
For the Lord blesses each of us with a Gift.

I can memorize dates to be exact.
I was born this way, for that is a fact.

I Beat At A Drum you're not familiar with.
For the Lord blesses each of us with a Gift.

I can use my skills to work at a job productively.
I just need a little assistance from those in my community.

I Beat At A Drum you're not familiar with.
For the Lord blesses each of us with a Gift.

You may hear a sound different from what you have known.
Please Hear and Listen.
For the Lord makes room for everyone.
I Beat At A Drum!

The Joy In The Morning

The sun can shine even if you don't see it.
The sun can shine in you.
Find the joy within no matter
What each new day will bring.
For there's always-
The Joy In The Morning!

Thank You For This Day

Dear Lord-
I thank you for this day.
This day as I begin a new found journey.
Full of the promise and the faith I have found
With you.
I thank you for each blessing you bestow upon me.
I sing with abounding joy of your love.
And as I awake each day,
I ask for your anointing—
Giving me the reassurance
That with your grace,
Your mercy,
I can always begin again.
Dear Lord-
I Thank You For This Day.

Road Blocks

As I keep going each day.
I am finding many Road Blocks along the way.

Whether I go left or right.
Going forward—traveling day or night.

The Road Blocks are always there.
Feeling helpless, and in despair.

Frustrated!
Not knowing what to do.
I remember that Prayer is the answer,
And I come to know the Lord
Will see me through.

And as I journey on—I continue on with the
Many Road Blocks along the way.
And again, I remember to Pray.

For the Lord is never forsaking.
He gives me strength,
And I stay strong.
And as He sees me through—I continue on.
For there are many-
Road Blocks!

The Morning Sun

Revelations came to me
At the break of dawn.
Realizing many things.
Looking over my life,
How it has been,
Where I am now,
And where I am going.
Letting go of issues from others,
Issues I have, I'm facing
What I can't change.
And I'm moving forward to a new change.
My healing begins.
And I can see clear,
As I see-
The Morning Sun

Hope

Giving up is surrender to no place.
When all seems lost, holding on
Brings you one step closer to the promise.
And as you believe each day is a new day,
Your trials can be your triumph.
Just believe that it all gets better,
No matter your circumstance,
No matter what you go through.
Believe what is now can change tomorrow.
Believe with Faith.
And always hold on to-
Hope.

Don't Forget To Count Your Blessings

When at times things are not going right.
Just remember to hold on to the good things
In your life.
Don't Forget To Count Your Blessings

When there are those you find
Do not think of you.
Remember the ones who do.
Don't Forget To Count Your Blessings

When you find the world is not kind.
Look for the "rainbow" in the sky-
And know you will be fine.
Don't Forget To Count Your Blessings

And when you cannot find what you are looking for-
Look around.
And be thankful the Lord has for you-
Greater things in store.
Don't Forget To Count Your Blessings!

The Joy In The Morning

Life has its storms.
And there's always the joy in the morning
That can carry you through the night,
And the next day,
And after that.
When problems arise,
And there seems no relief.
Hold on to the joy!
Let the sun shine through.
Believe it all takes care of itself,
No matter the storm.
And you'll find peace.
For Life has its Storms.
And there's always-
The Joy In The Morning!

I Have A Song In My Heart

I hear the birds Sing.
I receive the Lord's Blessing.
Oh! How beautiful the Sound.
God's presence is all around.

I sing no sad song.
Unhappiness does not last long.
With such joyful tears,
I've learned through the years.

Life is precious and worth living.
The best of me I keep giving.
I trust in God always.
Peace, Joy, and Love I carry with me
The rest of my days.
For-
I Have A Song In My Heart

A New Day Begins

Each new day can bring challenges as well as the joys.
Sometimes the rain comes to make room
For the sun to shine even brighter.
For life is forever changing—And A New Day Begins.

Each Time—There's A Blessing

Sometimes things doesn't always
Turn out the way we hope.
And sometimes they do.
But remember for every situation-
There's a Blessing through it all.
For through the most difficult times,
His love, His mercy is there for you always.

When it seems that hope is all gone,
Believe and hold on to Him evermore.
For every storm passes,
And a new day begins.
For-
There's Always A Blessing—*Each Time*

Reminders

There'll always be reminders
Of what's long past.
Surfacing over and over again.
Reflections of distant memories,
And what is now.
Reminders as one's life changes,
Growth can be a challenge,
And the will to survive is a test
Of the spirit.
Reminders to say it's ok
To look back without living there.
To move on, and to let go.
Reminders to understand what
Was, is not now to live,
And always to learn.
While the pages of life's experiences
Continue to turn.
There'll always be-
Reminders.

I Cannot Stay Where I Am

This change I find in me,
Empowers me to never give up,
To endure,
With Faith.
And whatever obstacles along the way,
I can overcome.
Today I own this for self,
And go forward with a new vision
To know all things I dream for,
Hope for,
I can achieve.
I cannot stay where I am.
And I Thank you Lord For This.

Foundation

Rebuilding—starting over
With dreams set in motion,
There's a life to get back.
Reorganizing and going another direction,
There's a feeling this time it will be different.
This time it will be better.
And as one storm has passed,
Then before you know comes another one.
But this time it's different.
And as the peace within you overflows,
Prosperity is not far off.
Rebuilding—starting over
With dreams set in motion.
There's a life to get back.
My Life!

Life Has Its Seasons

For as each season turns—so does life.
There'll be moments of joy
On any given day.
And there'll be moments of sorrow.
There'll be a time to heal,
And a time to pray.
Life Has Its Seasons.

There'll be moments to prosper,
And there can be moments of hardship,
And great loss.
A time to rebuild
What has been torn down.
A time to start over.
Life Has Its Seasons.

There'll be moments to gather together,
And there'll moments to be alone,
Until the time to come together again.
While there'll be moments to celebrate
For whatever the occasion brings.
Life Has Its Seasons.

There'll be moments of joy
On any given day.
And there'll be moments of sorrow.
There'll be a time to heal,
And a time to pray.
For each season turns-
So does *Life*.
Life Has Its Seasons.

I Wish To Live Life

I want to receive the Lord's Blessings every day.
I want to be at my best,
Even if I'm at my worst in every way.

I want to hold on to only good feelings in my heart.
I want to move on from disappointments
As I make a new start.

I want to be receptive of change,
And not loose me.
I want to always in every situation,
Open my eyes and see.

I want to look back at the past to reflect,
And not feel sorrow.
I want to hold on to hope
As I look forward to tomorrow.

I want to always to "keep the faith"
For dreams to come true.
I want to not remain sad, lonely, and blue.

I want to always let positive thinking
In my life play a vital part.
And-
I want to always have *Love* in my heart.
For-
I Wish To Live Life!

Start Anew

When you start anew,
Just remember to keep you.
For each situation you journey is different.
And each one you meet is not the same.
Go into each experience leaving issues
Of the heart behind.
Let positive thoughts fill your mind.
Forgive, even if it's hard to do.
And just let Love take you,
When you-
Start Anew

Morning

Yesterday has come and gone.
Tomorrow brings promise,
And always hope.
And for now,
I'm doing alright.
Yes! I'm doing just fine.
And each breath I take,
It's Good.
Yes! It's All Good!
Hello-
Morning!

A New Day Begins

Life is always changing-
And a new day begins.
Life has its challenges,
Its joys.
The good news is while
You're here there's always
The opportunity to live
Each day as if it's your last.
Take each experience
And always see the blessing
Behind every one.
Sometimes things don't always
Work out as we hope.
But never give up on Hope.
Sometimes the rain comes
To make room for the sun to shine
Even brighter.
For life is always changing-
And-
A New Day Begins!

This Day Today

This day today,
I took a moment to breathe,
To laugh,
And to smile.

This day today,
I saw hope through the disappointments.
To stay always encouraged.

This day today,
I focused on the goodness.
To know all gets better if one believes.

This day today,
I practiced the act of Faith,
To keep going,
To never give up.

This day today,
I took a moment to breathe,
To laugh,
To smile,
And to Pray!
This Day Today!

Accepting

Let go of what you cannot change.
The change starts with you.
Let go and let love take you.
For as you do this- you'll find
That with acceptance comes - Peace.

Forgive

O Lord! Teach me how to forgive.
Show me the way to Love, a better way to live.

Lord! Sometimes I get confused,
And I'm not sure which way to go.

I lay my troubles on your shoulders,
Please help me to grow.

Dear Lord!
There are times when the world is unkind,
And I find myself in despair.

Please anoint me with your love.
Even when the world seems to not care.

Direct me in a positive way,
So I can be example of goodness and grace.

I only want to know your way,
To guide me to the right place.
Dear Lord!
Please teach me how to-
Forgive.

A New Day

I awake from a long sleep,
Yes a long sleep from loneliness,
Self pity,
And regret.
I no longer choose to taste the bitter tongue
Of the trials of life.

I no longer allow worry, self-doubt,
And negative energy to be the focus of existence.
I no longer starve for others approval,
Opinions, and love.

Forgiveness is what I practice.
Patience has become my daily routine.
Love keeps me alive.
And I seek Him always.
As I Start-
A New Day

Whirlwind

In a whirlwind spinning
Out of control.
Finally stepping back
To see what direction
You're taking.
Is it good?
Is it right?
Understanding what is meant to be.
Revaluating all of it since it started,
And where it is now.
Then to realize for self,
That Acceptance is Peace.

Letting Go

Cleansing in one's soul.
Peace,
And serenity flows.
Hurt,
And pain released.
Your heart at peace.
Love steps in,
As you surrender it to Him.
Letting Go!

I Do Not Want To Hurt Anymore

I'm afraid.
Why?
I have been hurt.
And it seems as though things don't change.
What to do?

I feel at times I want to go away, and hide.
Still I find that is not the answer.
Should I just avoid situations with those who can be cruel?
Still I find that is not the answer.
Should I just cry?
Oh but that would make me sad.
And I have been there before.
Or should I just be mad?
And I have been there before too.
And I was unhappy.
And yet, I'm still afraid.
So I Pray! And I Pray! And I Pray!

Maybe if I just learn to like myself.
I may come to see that I am someone.
Then maybe I can believe everything
Will be just fine.
For-
I Do Not Want To Hurt Anymore

Surrender

May the peace fill your inner soul,
No matter life's trials and tribulations.

May the peace give you strength
To continue on each day with hope.

May the peace sustain you through
The most difficult times of your life.

May the peace give you faith to know
That all works out in time.

And as you surrender it all to Him-
May the peace stay with you now-
And each and everyday.

Take Me To Your Place

Touch me My Father!
Shower me with your
Goodness and grace.
Help me stay still in times of trouble,
And for whatever trials I may face.
Take Me To Your Place

Strengthen me in the Spirit,
So your voice is the only voice I hear.
Stay with me, and talk to me,
Whether it be far or near.
Take Me To Your Place

Anoint me!
Lift me up in your spirit.
Help me accept and love others for
Who they are.
Grant me everlasting peace.
And if I stray Lord too far!—
Take Me To Your Place!

Peace

Sometimes forgiving can be difficult,
Especially when feeling hurt and disappointed.
Sometimes even when the world is unkind,
Being right doesn't hold too much.
Letting go can be such a wonderful feeling,
And the world will seem much nicer.
It's a matter of perspective.
It's a matter how to deal with it
In your mind—in your heart—in your soul.
To let go with no hesitation for the simple
Reason to be at-
Peace

Accepting

Healing from the hurt and pain.
I cry no tears like rain.
I Am—Accepting

Letting go of things that don't change.
Cleaning out the junk in my heart-
Only to rearrange.
I Am—Accepting

To Rearrange! To Rearrange!
Putting things in priority.
Seeing Blessings, and no excess baggage I carry.
I Am—Accepting

Moving away from disappointments.
Picking up the broken pieces to begin again.
Never giving up on life.
Loving who I am.
Believing I am my best friend.
I Am—Accepting

Not wearing a frown.
Carrying only a smile.
Giving my worries to God.
And all the while.
I Am-
Accepting

New Life

As I move towards a new way of thinking-
Positive—leaving all old habits
Of negativity behind me.

I discover new oceans with a sense of direction.
Going forward I can plainly see.

The Sunset, the Blue Skies-
Oh! How beautiful it is to see God's creation.
For life is so precious
To waste even a minute
Of its treasures to go by.

As I stop and take time to smell the Roses-
I have a smile on my face with love
In my heart for others,
For this I must try.

In knowing I can always begin again.
In an effort towards being the best I can be.
To seek salvation-
To live a better way.

And as I find I have complete serenity
Within my heart-
For then I can say-
This is a wonderful-
New Life.

God's Peace

When the world seems too much to bear,
Too much to grasp—I look up to know that
He's always there. With Him such peace—I find.

May Each Day Lord I See You

Lord!-
May each day I see only you when trouble comes.
May each day I see only you when it seems no hope.
May each day I see only you
When the world is not at its best.
May each day I see only you
When sorrow is all around.

May each day I see your goodness
And grace shine throughout
As the morning comes,
As the noon day appears,
And as the evening makes its way
Before I lay down to sleep.

And Dear Lord!-
May your peace spread through every
River, ocean, mountain, hilltop,
And every shore—
For all to see and know.
Dear Lord!-
May Each Day I See You!

Avenues

Alone I walk in the morning sun,
I find there're many roads to venture to.
Not sure where I'm going,
For there're many directions
To follow through.

With so much before me,
I find things can change
From one minute to the next.
And I'm learning life
Is all about passing the test.

I ask the Lord to be my teacher.
I ask the Lord to be my guide.
And no matter what my life may be-
I feel His Love inside.

Alone I walk in the morning sun,
I find there're many roads to venture to.
Not sure where I'm going,
For there're many directions
To follow through.
There Are Many-
Avenues

The Lord Watches Over Me

I do not fear the darkness at night.
For the sparrow stays within my sight.
Oh! How The Lord Watches Over Me.

I do not fear the arrows that come at me
During the day.
For the Lord is all around,
He is with me in every way.
The Lord Watches Over Me.

I do not dwell too long in despair.
For I know I am in the Lord's care.
The Lord He Watches Over Me.

I trust in the Lord, I hold on to his
Unchanging hand.
For when I am weak, He helps me stand.
The Lord Watches Over Me.

I will stay in the house of the Lord,
He will never leave me.
For I know with Faith,
He is with me through eternity.
Oh! How The Lord Watches Over Me.

On My Journey

On My Journey
I've traveled many places, and I've learned
So much, and yet—I'm still learning.

On My Journey
I've experienced disappointments, as well as triumphs.
I've found me, and I'm happy with what I've found.

On My Journey
I've found that things can change, even with the same
Situation, and that nothing is complete, or certain.

On My Journey
I've discovered that no matter what others opinions may be,
One has to make choices which are best for them.

On My Journey
I've opened my mind to see the goodness in others,
Letting go of what I can't change,
Finding where I need to be.

On My Journey
I've traveled many places, and I've learned
So much.
And yet-
I'm Still Learning!

The Beauty Of Love

As you love, you live fulfilled.
And as you give love, you encourage
Others to give too.
But remember, there're times when love
May not be accepted or received by some.
And sometimes you may feel if it's worth the try.
But just stop and think
As you turn a negative situation
To a positive one,
You'll find much peace, much joy
You can ever imagine when you always
Answer to your heart.
Can you ever imagine anything greater?
For that's-
The Beauty of Love

Home

Balancing it all together,
What makes sense is the
Purpose of why I'm here.
Where I am meant to be-
At peace always,
In my soul always.
And yes,
Love I find everywhere.
While other things come and go,
Love never dies!
I see the morning sun,
I start a new day.
And it's all because of you.
You have given me new life.
More greater than I can ever imagine.
It never left me.
Though at times I've moved away from it.
And this is where I will stay.
So glad I found my way back—here.
Dear Lord!
So glad I'm-
Home.

My Prayer For You

I pray His Love will shower upon you each day.
May his arms surround you,
To encourage you through your travels,
To comfort you when you need a friend,
To guide and sustain you through the most
Difficult times.

May you find joy as the morning comes.
And may it stay with you as the sun goes down,
To hold you to the new day at the break of dawn.

I pray His Love shower upon you each day
Of your life.
May His Love be with you always.

God's Peace

When the world seems too much to bear-
Too much to grasp,
I seek your peace within.
I find your strength to sustain me at all times.
And I pray more than ever before.
For it's your peace that flows like
The water along any brook or stream.
It's your peace that makes the new fallen snow
So beautiful on a brisk winter's morning.
It's your peace when the birds sing so lovely
On a warm summer's day.
It's your peace when the leaves fall
So gently in October.
It's your peace so beautiful.
When the world seems too much to bear-
Too much to grasp,
I look up to know you're always there.
With you-
Such Peace-
I Find.

Fulfillment

There are those moments we may find
We're not where we should be.
The good news is-
As you work towards what you can change
Always in you, such peace you'll find.
For to walk with Him only gets better
Each day you breathe life.
And as you leave behind
The old life you once knew,
Welcoming the new life,
Nourishing your soul
With his love,
That lifts you up.
Such blessings overflow,
Encouraging you to continue on the journey
He has in place for you.
Always to be-
Fulfilled.

In Due Season

You cannot go back to where you were,
Nor can you stay where you are.
But as you go forward your faith is renewed,
And all things are possible within the deepest
Desires of your heart.

Possibilities

Hold on to your dreams
For the possibility to come true.
Never stop believing for a Blessing may come to you.
And if you find your dreams
You reach for seem impossible to achieve.
Continue to hold on to your dreams,
And Believe.
Hold on to-
Possibilities!

Loving You

Have love for others,
Give the best of you.
Stand up for what you believe in,
Just remain true.

Don't be persuaded by others
To change who you are.
Find your gift,
Learn to fly,
And you'll go far.

For life's greatest gift
Is to believe in what you can do.
Knowing you have something
That is only unique to you.
For It Is All About-
Loving You

A Journey Of A Thousand Steps

You must never give up when it seems so far.
You must never doubt when it all seems it's going nowhere.
You must never say you can't-always say you can.
It doesn't matter how long the journey.
What matters that you give it your all,
All the way to the end.
A true winner never gives up,
Never doubts when things go wrong,
Always gearing with positive energy,
No matter how the road turns.
For one single step leads to a thousand steps,
Making dreams come true.

As I Plant The Seeds Of My Garden

As I Plant the Seeds of My Garden,
I plant my goals, my dreams,
And my visions of all I wish to do.
I cultivate the many goals,
I work towards to pursue.

As I Plant the Seeds of My Garden,
I vision my dreams blossoming with
Many opportunities.
And with self-determination,
My visions become a reality.

As I Plant the Seeds of My Garden,
I'm learning in accomplishing great
Achievements,
And Success,
Comes Courage,
And the belief in You!

I plant my goals,
My dreams,
And my visions.
Making them possible to become true.
As I Plant the Seeds of My Garden.

The Comfort Zone

Great achievements does not come easy.
Sometimes you have to venture out
Of the Comfort Zone.

The journey may seem long,
And you may wonder the dreams you set
Will come to surface.

Oh! The comfort zone where all is good
And comfortable-
Why should one leave chasing rainbows?

But that's the joy of it all.
Visualizing your dreams to come true.
Visualizing what you can achieve,
If you only believe,
And keep going with the persistence,
And faith.
Your dreams can come true.
Leaving-
The Comfort Zone

In Due Season

When I think about all the blessings
He brings.
When I think about His Grace—His Love,
I can only stay where he wants me to be.
I cannot doubt him,
No matter what,
No matter the challenges.
And when the storms come,
And it seems as though they will not pass,
I look up to Him to know
He's my help,
He's my friend.
And whatever my desires,
I know He will grant.
Yes,
Always-
In Due Season

Inspiration

To believe all is possible,
That seems impossible,
To always encourage,
To enlighten the spirit,
To spread a little love wherever you go.
And just maybe as you pass it on,
The world will be more beautiful,
And before you know what a difference
You've made.
A more beautiful world you can ever
Have dreamed.
If you could only imagine
Such an inspiration that would be?

Faith

Never stop believing and go with faith.
Hold on to the blessings He so brings.
For today may not be your tomorrow.

The Miracles of God

He sends his angels
To watch over you
As the morning comes,
The moment you awake,
And as you rest your eyes at night.
A miracle may come at any moment,
Of each day,
Anytime—
Anywhere.

Hold on to the hope,
His everlasting love.
And always—Pray.
May his peace fill you to know,
His angels may come in many ways.

An angel may come to encourage you
When you feel you can't go on.
An angel may come just to hold your hand
When you feel afraid.
An angel may come as an answer to a prayer
You asked for yesterday, and today.

An angel may come when one door closes,
Just for another door to open.
An angel may come when all hope seems lost,
But just over the horizon,
A light shines to bring you hope,
For today,
And tomorrow.
A Miracle happens!
Such are the wonderful-
Miracles of God!

Always With Hope

In Dedication To The Survivors of Breast Cancer

Always with Hope there's the reassurance
Things will get better.
And no matter what you're going through
At the moment,
No matter what trials you may endure-
It too will pass.

Always with Hope you're encouraged
To never stop believing,
You're encouraged to hold on
To the blessings He brings to you
On any given day.

Always with Hope
There's the reassurance
Things will get better-
Always With Hope

Believe what is now can change tomorrow.
Believe with faith,
And always hold on to—Hope.

To Fly Like An Eagle

To fly like an eagle
Is to follow one's dreams
For however long it takes you.
Always daring about new adventures beyond
Your imagination.

To fly like an eagle
Is never giving up when the distance seems so far.
Moving beyond the barriers, the obstacles.
Stead fast with self-determination.

To fly like an eagle
Is to believe you can do all you dream to be.
Keeping your spirits high with positive energy,
Always giving your best!

To fly like an eagle
Is believing each step you take,
Brings you closer that all is possible,
Beyond and Beyond!
Just Fly Like an Eagle!

Alone

Alone does not always stand for lonely,
Sometimes it's a great healing-
That space to grow.

Alone sometimes helps you with a great
Sense of focus and perspective.
And the trials can be triumphs.

Alone sometimes helps you stay encouraged,
Empowering you to many heights—many possibilities.

Alone is a period each of us experiences
For however long it may be.
Overcoming barriers-
Moving forward with belief in one's self.

Alone does not always stand for lonely,
For it can take you to other places,
Expanding your horizons,
And finding you're not-
Alone

Beginnings

Circumstances can change,
And as one moves on,
A new day begins.

Moving on with no fears,
No worries of what's ahead.
Just confidence and peace of mind
To know it will be alright.

Going forward,
Moving beyond where you are,
To where you need to be.
For each step you take with Faith,
Believe your dreams can come true.
And it's just the-
Beginning

The Leap Of Faith

Take the leap of faith and believe
Each step you take empowers you
To go the distance.
Find strength through each challenge
You so endure.
And when disappointments come,
Receive them as blessings
To keep going even more.
Never give up,
No matter what comes your way,
No matter how difficult the climb.
Just know as you keep going,
His Mercy,
His Love,
Will never fail you.
Take the Leap of Faith
And—
Believe

Each Day I Believe

For each moment of each day,
I Believe-
Always with the Faith,
Dreams do come true.

For each day I awake,
And each day I breathe life,
Those blessings he always brings
When you least expect,
Gives me hope,
To know all is possible when you just believe.

Each moment of each day,
And always with the Faith,
Each Day-
I Believe.

Winners

Winners see beyond the boundaries,
Always searching high.
Winners always say: "I can do it"-
Believing their dreams can come true.
Winners never quit.
They stay the distance all through the end.
Winners don't compare themselves to others.
Only strive for the best in themselves.
Winners live by courage, and faith,
Standing tall with a job well done.
Winners see beyond the boundaries,
Always searching high.
Shining beautiful like a Star!

Faith

It keeps you going forward.
With it—opportunities are yours to explore.
You can follow the desires deep within you.
You can overcome the barriers—the obstacles.
You can cross bridges that seem so far to reach.
You can climb any mountain.
And like an eagle you can fly high above the skies-
With Courage-
With Confidence-
With Strength-
With-
Faith

The Promise Of God

He always answers prayers.
For that's His promise.
Sometimes He answers prayers
Through the most simplest of things.
And sometimes he answers them
Through the winds of the world.

He doesn't always answer prayers
In the way we ask.
He doesn't always work in our time,
Always in His time.
Sometimes he appoints angels on earth
To fulfill his promise so dear.

He always hears our hearts,
And what we wish, and dream for to be.
He will never fail us,
Nor leave,
Nor forsake us.
And Yes!
He answers prayers.

When prayers go up to him,
He Hears,
He Listens,
With his everlasting Love.
He always knows what's best,
In every given moment of one's life.

For with Hope each day,
And abiding Faith,
He reassures and fulfills the promise
So True-
That He always answers-
Prayers.

Memories & Reflections

As I reflect of days passed,
I think of the wonderful times we've shared.
For every season that comes each year,
I cherish those memories of you.
Each season I'll think of you.

Daddy

In fond memory of my father William Buchanan Sr.

I have so many wonderful memories of so many things,
When you were in my life.
You and Mother raised seven children,
William, Larry, George,
Phillip, Joyce, Gloria, and me.
You were a *beacon of life.*

I can still hear you say: "Doris Jean,"
It's time to put the beans on."
Years have passed, and sometimes,
I still don't believe you're gone.

When I was a little girl in Louisville, Kentucky,
I remember the names you had for Joyce, Gloria, and me.
"Mamma Tub," "Mamma Pearl," "Kool-Aid,"
I'm not too sure which one was mine.
I do know they were given with love—all the time.

I can still see you and Aunt Mary fussing.
And how she used to tell you what to do.
And you would tell her a thing or too.

And then when we moved to Harrisburg, PA.
And no matter the time, you would sit
On the front porch everyday.
And when you came home from your job
At the Military Depot—you would give me a "wink of your eye."
And you were always cheering George on,
When he played football at *Old John Harris High.*

You were always kind to others,
And giving of your self.
And how you would take the time
To lend someone a hand-
Always ready to help.

You taught me about telling the truth
Is always the best way.
For all these things I remember so well,
Stay with me today.
And how you would wait up for me
When I came home late from those parties I went to.
For I was blessed to have a "Daddy"
Watching over me.
I was blessed to have you.

There were those who knew you as—Daddy Buck!
But for me—you'll always be-
Daddy

Mother, I Thank You

Mother, I Thank you-
For so much you have done for me.

Mother, I Thank you-
For believing in me to be the best I can be.

Mother, I Thank you-
For your Love, and how you care.

Mother, I Thank you-
For no matter what-you're always there.

Mother, I Thank you-
For showing me kindness,
Thoughtfulness,
And Grace.

Mother, I Thank you-
For no one can take your place.

Mother, I Thank you-
For instilling in me the importance of an education,
Following your dreams,
And much more.

Mother, I Thank you-
For a good example of what a—Mother is for.-
Mother, I Thank you.

Mother

You've shown me how to be strong through
Life's trials from day to day.
You've shown me that patience
Is learned through time,
And to welcome many of life's challenges
As they come my way.

You've shown me that people love differently
In their own way.
This I've come to see.
And most of all-
You've shown me
What a Mother is supposed to be.

Sisterly Love

A Love of acceptance the way you are,
Not always perfect and refined.
A love of differences of opinions,
As well as likes.
And a closeness the two of you share.
A love through miles and distance,
And always thoughts of each other is near.
A love to remind you of the bond you have
Of family ties forever in time.
A love where differences do not matter,
With the acceptance that disagreements you
Sometimes have.
A love where Love stays with you,
No matter your walk in life.
A love only sister's can share.
This Love-
Sisterly Love

Bryan

In Loving Memory of my nephew Bryan

When I see Love, I see no standards,
No judgments,
And no rules.
When I see Love,
I see a smile for no reason,
A burst of sunshine
When the sun is shining,
And when it's not.

When I see Love,
I see laughter for one's tears,
Comfort for one's pain,
And understanding when there's none.
When I see Love, I see the goodness in others,
And making room for their goodness to shine through.

When I see Love, I see being at your best,
Even when you're at your worst.
When I see Love, I see no conditions to Love,
And always having an open door
To the heart to Love.
When I see Love—I See-
Bryan

Blessings

The sun shining all the time
Life through devastation
Seeing a newborn child
Prayers answered over and over again
Giving life back
Finding peace
Children laughing and playing
A smile
Being In Love
Seizing the moments
The Love of a Mother
A Father's joy
A child's gift
Family Gatherings
Friendship
Seeing an old friend
Unexpected presents
A bouquet of flowers
Pink Roses
Snow on Christmas Day
Spring in Washington DC
A rainbow after the rain

Summer Breezes
A Thank you for no reason
Encouragement
Fulfillment
Inspirational messages
A pat on the back
A Hug
Congratulations
A listening ear
A helping hand
An understanding heart
Love-
Blessings!

Friends I Know

Fondly I say there are those friends I know-
Whose love is so wonderful to have in one's Life.
Those little things that we sometimes take
For granted, those friends I know—Do!

When those friends I know call me to see if I'm ok.
When those friends I know encourage me to
Never give up.

When those friends I know make me laugh
Through the sunshine,
And through the rain.
When those friends I know always have a listening ear.

When those friends I know don't mind my imperfections,
Just love me as I am.
When those friends I know take the time to get to know me,
Just to know me.

When those friends I know care,
And offer support and love.
Yes! I'm so glad I have in my life-
Those-
Friends I Know!

Thank You for All You Do

In honor of our Military Members of the Armed Forces of the United States of America

Thank you for all you do,
For all we stand for,
For America-
The Home of the Brave,
The Land of the Free.
For all we value-
Life,
Liberty,
And The Pursuit of Happiness.
Thank you for all you do,
Fighting in distant lands,
Proud to serve,
No matter where you are.
And when danger is upon you,
I pray that as you keep us safe,
The Lord keeps you safe,
Each day as the morning breaks,
When the sun sets,
And when nightfall approaches.

Thank you for all you do,
For every time you are away,
May we never forget
All that you do.
For all we stand for,
For America-
The Home of the Brave,
The Land of the Free,
For all we value,
Life,
Liberty,
And The Pursuit of Happiness-
Thank You For All You Do.

To Those Fathers I Know

They teach and instill responsibility,
Integrity,
And-
Respect.
They give their very best in all they do.
And when the time calls for it,
They never fall short of their commitments
To their family and their friends.
You can lean on them when you need
Advice and a listening ear—a shoulder to lean on.
Fathers are not just-
Football,
Baseball,
Or whatever the sport may be.
They are those heroes
Whose love speaks with a silent voice
Giving the best of themselves,
Living by what they teach-
Responsibility,
Integrity,
Respect-
And always their *Love* open wide.

The Small Blessings

Each day you awake be thankful
For every moment you have.
Each and every moment is a Blessing.
Take those moments
And make your own memories.
Let every moment count,
And make the best of what you have.

You are rich not for so much wealth
That you possess,
But more so what you do with what you have
To make it last.
Enjoy the time with the ones you love.
For Life is not promised to us.

Live each day full and not empty.
See the sunrise as the morning comes,
And watch the sunset as it calms the skies-
Over the horizon.
For right now is yours to live
To its fullest.
Have no regrets,
And enjoy the small blessings
With the reassurance they are
His gifts to us.

Each day you awake be thankful
For every moment you have.
Each and every moment is a—*Blessing.*

Friends

Friends encourage you to live your dreams,
Allow you to cry when you need to,
Laugh with you,
And hold your hand when you're afraid.
Friends always stay no matter the distance
And miles, no matter the years that pass.
For through this life,
You'll always have your-
Friends.

Best Wishes

I wish you well,
Good fortune,
And always the best.
And may you find much joy,
Much happiness-much love.
I wish you more days of sunshine,
And less days of rain.
And may you always be blessed
No matter where you go.
I wish you wonderful friends
To keep you encouraged.
And may the love of family,
And friends stay with you always.
I wish you well,
Good fortune,
And always the Best!

Memories

I'll think of you
As the winter snow falls at night,
And all is calm.
I'll think of you
As the flowers blossom,
Preparing for the spring.
I'll think of you
As autumn makes its way,
After long beautiful summer days.
I'll think of you
As seasons pass each year,
Reminding me of wonderful times
We've shared.
And now that you're with Him,
There'll always be the memories to cherish.
I'll think of you.

Family

Accepting each other with love abound,
And when distance surfaces,
There's the reminder that love is
Always there with no rules,
No conditions.
Even when time passes,
Not seeing each other for so long,
Till the time you come together,
Remembering those childhood days
With Daddy's and Mother's Love,
With brothers,
Sisters,
Aunts,
Uncles,
Cousins,
And grandparents,
Makes wonderful memories to cherish.
Accepting each other with love abound,
And when distance surfaces,
There's the reminder that love is always
There with no rules, no conditions.
There's always-
Family

A Time, A Season,
And Always Love

I pray more than ever now.
I pray for each season for love to stay.
For a revaluation of thoughts to see love
And believe in it so.
I pray for A Time, A Season, And-
Always Love.

Always With Love

There's nothing greater than Love.
For throughout time—*Love* last.
One can have all the faith,
And believe all things are possible,
But without *Love* nothing matters.
One can have enormous wealth,
And give it all way,
But without Love it has no value.

Love allows the heart to give without seeking,
Love allows the heart to forgive without bitterness.
Love allows the heart to see with no jealousy
Envy,
Paranoia-
Only the truth.
Love allows the heart to understand with
Tolerance,
Understanding,
And-
Compassion.
For Love stands throughout time.
There's nothing greater than *Love.*

For as one heart sees with *Love,*
It encourages another heart,
And another heart too!
Love will always withstand all things.
And the world will be a more beautiful place.
Yes! A more beautiful place we could ever have dreamed-
Always—With Love!

Walls

Walls divide us, separate us, and keep us away.
Love has no place to stay.
Walls limit us to only go so far.
They stagnate us from being who we are.

Walls promote ignorance,
And encourage discrimination.
Differences are not welcomed,
Leaving not much room for communication.

Walls block understanding from coming in.
They breathe prejudice outwardly,
And within.

Walls keep our spirits dormant.
They do not allow us to trust.
They close our hearts to where we don't give
The best of us.

Walls—Divide! Divide! Divide!
And behind them we hide.

Walls—For if we bring them down.
Love! Love! Love!
Will stay around.
Walls!

Love

It's everywhere.
It solves every problem.
It resolves conflict.
It makes a way for every solution.
It doesn't discriminate or judge.
It brings people together.
We can't live without it.
We may turn away from it.
We may cover it over with things.
And sometimes we may not see it
When it comes.
But-
If we step back, we can see it so clear.
We can see it through the smiles and the hugs.
We can see it through encouragement.
We can see it through a listening ear.
We can see it through the support of a friend,
Especially when we need it the most.
We can see it through patience, and understanding.
We can see it through kindness, and compassion.
Yes—We can see it.
It's Everywhere.
It's-
Love

Only Love

Love is the answer to all things.
For as one heart that has love,
Inspires many hearts to know love.
Love is far better to have than
All the wealth,
The fame,
And statue in life.
Only Love can conquer all.
Love can change the world
Beyond imagination—
A more beautiful world we
Could ever have dreamed.
Love forgives,
Listens,
And hears with the heart.
There's nothing that can surpass Love.
Love is the answer to all things.
Only—Love

The Christian Walk

Each day I would like to take the Christian Walk,
To remember what Jesus was all about.
Each day I would like to be an example
Of His Grace,
To be honest, sincere,
And true.
To give more than receive.
To offer my hand to someone without question.
To always seek in my heart compassion, tolerance,
And understanding.

Each day I would like to take the Christian Walk,
To take responsibility for my wrongs.
To not judge others for their shortcomings.
To be more forgiving,
To stand tall with love when I see wrong.
To find peace when all seems not at peace,
And to pray at all times with a humble heart.

Yes! I would like to take the Christian Walk,
Carrying *Love* in my heart always.
Just to know what Jesus is all about.

What Is A Christian Woman?

A Christian Woman praises the Lord
Through her trials, and through her joys.
She looks for the good in others.
She forgives a thousand times over.
She makes no list of wrongs.
She opens the door to understanding.
She listens and hears with love.
She finds peace through the suffering, and the pain.
She lives her days blessed.
She never forgets her family commitments.
She speaks truthfully her opinions with kindness,
And resolve.
She lives with compassion
No matter her circumstance.
She prays with a humble heart, without ceasing,
And always with Faith.
A Christian Woman is a doer,
And believer of the Word.
She's always giving of her heart.

A Man Who Is Rich

A Man Who is Rich-
Does not concern himself with success,
And wealth, he gives only the best of himself.

A Man Who is Rich-
Does not care so much about position, or material things.
He values his family, his job, and his friends.

A Man Who is Rich-
Does not forget his responsibilities.
He lives by truth, and integrity.

A Man Who is Rich-
Does not exclude himself from the world around him.
He expands himself to many, and gains the respect of his friends.

A Man Who is Rich-
Does not allow himself to be cynical, bitter, or unkind.
He thrives on positive thinking, he keeps an open mind.
A Man Who Is Rich-
Does not think selfish, or boast about what he does.
He finds fulfillment by doing what is right.
Filling his heart with Love.
For he has all these qualities, and more.
A Man Who Is Rich!

All Of A Sudden

Children will no longer be killing children.
All Of A Sudden

Families will spend more time together, not apart.
All Of A Sudden

People will start to talk, and not argue.
All Of A Sudden

Police will serve and protect all their citizens,
No matter race or disability.
All Of A Sudden

There will be no more hunger in the land.
All Of A Sudden

There will be a cure for cancer, and the sick will
Have hope.
All Of A Sudden

All of us will have a better quality of life.
All Of A Sudden

There will be no more hate—only love.

For before you know it—God's Love
Will conquer all.
All Of A Sudden!

Where The Grass Is Green

There has to be a place—Where the Grass Is Green,
Where Love is—always love.

There has to be a place—Where the Grass is Green,
Where I can be me,
And not concern myself if it's ok.

There has to be a place—Where the Grass is Green,
Where patience lies,
And positive energy spreads in every direction.

There has to be a place—Where the Grass is Green,
Where there's no fear to live each day,
And to trust is common practice.

There has to be a place—Where the Grass is Green,
Where the quality of life is abundant,
And working hard has more value.

There has to be a place—Where the Grass is Green,
Where war is just a distant memory of
Yesterday,
And peace is something we don't have to
Dream about.

There has to be a place—Where the Grass is Green,
Where Love keeps growing,
Crushing hate to the ground.

There has to be a place—Where the Grass is Green,
Where love is—*Always Love.*
There has to be a place-
Where The Grass Is Green.

What Matters Is Love

What matters is what's in your heart.
For it's all about Love.
Just to keep it with you always.
To see with compassion, mercy,
Tolerance and understanding.
For it's all about Love.

What matters is to be ready to forgive,
Even when the heart is tired and weary,
And to stand no matter your trails, no matter your
Circumstance,
No matter your position with the Grace of God.
For it's all about Love.

What matters is to know the respect you give to others,
Will also come back to you.
And to pray at all times, even if you feel there's no
Love around.
For it's all about Love.
What matters is giving always with a humble heart,
Placing less value on things,
And more value into helping others.
For it's all about Love.
Yes!
What matters is what's in your heart.
For it's all about Love!

Choices

We can choose to be negative,
Or we can choose to be positive.
We can live in darkness,
Or we can turn on the light if we so choose.

We can choose to follow our dreams,
Or we can choose not to.
We can limit ourselves to go only so far,
Or we can seek our desires to endless possibilities
If we so choose.

We can make our own truth with
Jealousy, envy, and paranoia,
Or we can open our minds to the truth
If we so choose.

We can choose to be at war,
Or we can choose to be at peace.
We can harvest the seeds of ignorance and hate,
Or we can harvest the seeds of love if we so choose.

We choose the directions we take in our lives!
We choose the directions we take in our lives!
We Make Our Own-
Choices!

A Time, A Season, And Always Love

I pray more than ever now,
At a time where perceptions,
And what's on the surface
Has more weight, I pray for Love.

I pray for a revaluation of thoughts
To see love, and believe in it so.

For each season,
Each winter as the snow falls,
Each spring as the flowers blossom,
And the trees grow,
Each summer as more sunny
And warm days appear,
Each fall as the leaves fall,
And the cool winds fill the air,
I pray for each time,
Each season for love to stay.

I pray for a time where the act of trust,
And faith in humankind becomes more present,
Especially now.

I pray for Love to stay always,
Yes! Always!

I Pray for-
A Time, A Season, And Always Love.

The Lord's Grace

There's nothing like the Lord's Grace.
A feeling within your soul-
A journey to the right place.

A feeling of negativity to no longer
Enter your mind.
True goodness, righteousness,
And always love you will find.

For no matter where you are,
His Love is always around.
And with His Love, it lifts you up in spirit,
You're heavenly bound.

It is a journey towards true salvation
For the rest of your days.
For the Lord's Grace is a feeling of *Love*-
In your heart always.
For there's nothing like-
The Lord's Grace

Fri / 9:00 - 11:00 St. Luke C Church
11:30
4925 East Capitol St SE
Washington DC

CPSIA information can be obtained at www.ICGtesting.com
Printed in the USA
LVOW041439210312

274154LV00010B/9/P